Happy Entertaining!

Best Wishes,

Andy   Aug 94

Quick and Easy Menus for Entertaining

John

Merry Christmas 1994.

Love,

Mom

Quick and Easy Menus for Entertaining

SECRETS OF A SAVVY COOK

by Andy King

Photographs by Monte Bancroft

Abbeville Press   Publishers
New York London Paris

Editor: Ann ffolliott
Designer: Amanda Wilson
Production Editor: Renée Klock
Production Supervisor: Simone René

Food photography by Monte Bancroft
Cover photography by Jon Roemer
Food styling by Elizabeth Fassberg

Printed and bound in Singapore.

Library of Congress
Cataloging-in-Publication Data

King, Andy, 1961–
Quick and easy menus for
entertaining : secrets of a savvy
cook / by Andy King.
    p.   cm.
ISBN 1-55859-427-2 : $15.95
1. Entertaining.   2. Quick and easy
cookery.   3. Menus.   I. Title.
    TX731.K52   1994
642'.4 – dc20   94-6341
                                      CIP

Acknowledgments

• Bricettis Bedford Market
  Bedford Hills, New York

• Eclectic Interiors Inc.
  Bedford Hills, New York

• Dansk Factory Outlet &
  Dansk International Designs Ltd.
  Mount Kisco, New York

• Flickware by
  Geoffrey Flickinger Ceramics
  South Salem, New York

• L. H. Greene Inc. Florist
  Pound Ridge, New York

• Perennial Gardens
  Bedford, New York

Special Thanks to

Kent and Jennifer Sednaouy

Susie and Fred Bancroft

Ginger and Lee Getz

Arden Sperry, for her generosity
with time and patience

Mom and Bill, for their moral
support and enthusiasm

CONTENTS

INTRODUCTION

If necessity is the mother of invention, this book is the child of my own experience. Before beginning my life in the kitchen, I had a high-pressure job that included the entertainment of clients after regular office hours. Rather than the usual expense-account meal in a restaurant, I discovered that clients felt flattered when I invited them to share the hospitality of my bachelor's apartment. After working a ten-hour day, I frequently had six to ten guests for dinner. So I quickly learned to improvise and cut corners in food preparation, and to do so with flair.

Both clients and friends asked "How can you create such a spectacular meal in such a short time and with so little effort? What are your secrets?" The answer for them, and for you, is **Quick and Easy Menus for Entertaining: Secrets of a Savvy Cook.**

Now don't let the title fool you into thinking this is a gourmet cooking guide. It is for all people who may lack confidence in their entertaining skills. In other words, **Secrets of a Savvy Cook** presents easy meals that anyone can cook. Unlike most cookbooks, this one is designed specifically to show you how to create great meals using simple methods. While your guests are enjoying these meals, they will think you spent hours preparing the food. In reality, most meals in this book take only minutes to make.

The fear of failure is the biggest problem most people have in the kitchen. The shortcut recipes presented here make failure practically impossible, and they will enable you to conquer that fear. The truth is that it's not going to make a big difference if you happen to add a tablespoon of basil instead of a teaspoon, or $\frac{1}{4}$ cup of diced onion instead of $\frac{1}{2}$ cup. Further, it's hard to make a mistake when you are using prepared ingredients and all you have to do is mix them together.

Another problem for inexperienced cooks is knowing which foods go with what. **Secrets of a Savvy Cook** teaches you how to assemble a complete meal. Because this book is in menu form, you will see what goes well together, from appetizers to desserts. It will also show you how to improvise when needed; how to make do with what you have; and how to make it all taste good and look elegant. Soon you too will be able to throw a great party, large or small. It's easier than you think.

YOUR KITCHEN

I would like to take this time to introduce you to your kitchen–you know, that room in your house that you hate to go into. It's the one with all the empty cabinets and drawers. It's that place you go when you are hungry and throw something into the oven, microwave, or boiling water.

Let me show you a few things you can do there. You may say, "Wait a minute, I don't have a lot of time, money, or imagination!" That's not a problem, because there are plenty of menus in this book that will fit your needs. Some are simple and some are fancy, but all of them are easy to make.

Let's start with a few important tools. Don't worry about what's not on hand. Make do now, and slowly accumulate things you need.

**THINGS THAT GO
IN DRAWERS**

1 Spatula
1 Large wooden spoon
1 Large serving spoon
1 Large slotted spoon
1 Whisk
1 Vegetable peeler
1 Can opener
1 Bottle opener
1 Set of measuring spoons
1 Large sharp knife
1 Small sharp knife
1 Large serrated knife
1 Apple corer

**THINGS THAT GO
IN CABINETS**

Small, medium, and large
frying pans
Small, medium, and large
boiling pots
1 Steamer
2 Cookie sheets
1 Small and 1 large baking dish
1 Set of mixing bowls
1 Salad bowl and tongs

SEASONINGS

Granulated sugar

Brown sugar

Dried dill

Dried rosemary

Dried tarragon

Dried thyme

Curry powder

Sesame seeds

Ground cumin

Ground cinnamon

Dried mint leaves

Salt and pepper

MISCELLANEOUS ITEMS

Dishwasher detergent

Paper towels

Plastic wrap

Aluminum foil

Waxed paper

Zippered plastic bags

Sherry

White wine

Red wine

ESSENTIAL FOOD ITEMS

Soups

Cream of mushroom

Cream of chicken

Cream of asparagus

Chicken broth

Beef broth

Lobster bisque

Dried onion soup mix

Sauces, Dressings, and Accompaniments

Mayonnaise

Dijon mustard

Soy sauce

Tabasco sauce

Honey

Salad dressings

Maple syrup

Olive oil

Wine vinegar

Chutney

Starches

Assorted pastas

Rice

Potatoes

Bread

Stuffing mix

Bread crumbs

Dairy Products

Eggs

Milk

Butter

Cream

Margarine

Cream cheese

Sour cream

Ice cream

Vegetables

Frozen chopped spinach

Frozen whole green beans

Frozen tiny peas

Frozen corn

Carrots

Onions

Garlic

Fruits

Lemons

Limes

Apples

Small bunch of bananas

Canned mandarin oranges

Stuffed Mushroom Caps   Beef Stroganoff

Buttered Noodles   Tomatoes Stuffed with Spinach Soufflé

Blueberry Turnovers with Vanilla Ice Cream

FIRST SNOW

There's something special about sitting in front of a roaring fire and enjoying a simple dinner with good friends. Serve the dinner on a card table in front of the fire or sit around a coffee table on the floor. Use some of the wine in cooking and serve the rest. What a great way to spend a cold winter night!

SHOPPING LIST

1 2-pound (900 g) boneless steak
2 sweet Italian sausage links
12 fresh medium-large
   mushrooms
4 ripe medium tomatoes
1 small bunch fresh parsley
2 ounces (50 g) Parmesan cheese
   for grating
½ pint (250 ml) sour cream
1 10-ounce (280 g) package frozen
   spinach soufflé
4 frozen blueberry turnovers
1 pint (500 ml) vanilla ice cream
2 3-ounce (85 g) cans sliced
   mushrooms
1 10¾-ounce (300 g) can condensed
   cream of mushroom soup
1 1-pound (450 g) package
   egg noodles
1 1-ounce (30 g) envelope dried
   onion soup mix
1 to 2 bottles (750 ml) dry red wine

Staples
Flour
Italian-seasoned bread crumbs
Salt
Pepper
Butter (½ stick, 60 g)

Stuffed Mushroom Caps

12 medium-large mushrooms
2 sweet Italian sausage links
¼ cup (25 g) Italian-seasoned
   bread crumbs
¼ cup (30 g) grated
   Parmesan cheese

1. Preheat the broiler. Wipe the mushrooms with a damp paper towel and break off stems. Hollow out mushroom caps by flattening the insides.

Preparation time: 20 minutes

2. Slice each sausage link into 6 pieces. Place a slice of sausage inside each cap, then sprinkle with some bread crumbs and Parmesan cheese. Pack tightly and smooth the tops. Place in a broiling pan and broil until the sausage is cooked and no longer pink, about 5 minutes.

Preparation time: 25 minutes

Beef Stroganoff

1 2-pound (900 g) boneless
   steak (London Broil is
   inexpensive and flavorful
   but can be tough)
½ cup (90 g) all-purpose
   flour
2 tablespoons (30 g) butter
1 cup (250 ml) dry red wine
1 10¾-ounce (300 g) can
   condensed cream of
   mushroom soup
1 1-ounce (30 g) envelope
   dried onion soup mix
2 3-ounce (85 g) cans sliced
   mushrooms
½ pint (250 ml) sour cream
Salt and pepper

1. Cut the steak into thin strips and dredge in flour. Heat the butter in a large skillet and sauté the meat over high heat until brown and crisp, about 5 minutes.

2. Combine the wine and mushroom soup, then pour the mixture into the pan. Add 1 cup of water and the onion soup mix. Stir, reduce heat to low, and simmer for 25 minutes.

3. Drain the mushrooms and add to the pan. Remove pan from heat and slowly add the sour cream. Season to taste and serve with noodles.

Preparation time: 40 minutes

Buttered Noodles

1 1-pound (450 g) package
  egg noodles
2 tablespoons (30 g) butter
¼ cup (10 g) chopped
  fresh parsley

1. Follow directions on package for cooking noodles.

2. Drain in a colander and rinse with fresh water. Place noodles back in pot and add butter and parsley. Stir to blend well.

Preparation time: 15 minutes

Tomatoes Stuffed with Spinach Soufflé

1 10-ounce (300 g) package
  frozen spinach soufflé
4 medium tomatoes
About 2 tablespoons (15 g)
  grated Parmesan cheese
About 2 tablespoons (12 g)
  Italian-seasoned bread
  crumbs

1. Thaw the spinach soufflé. Preheat the oven to 350° F (180° C).

2. Cut the tops off the tomatoes and hollow out the insides.

3. Fill with spinach soufflé, then sprinkle the tops with Parmesan cheese and bread crumbs. Place in a baking dish and bake for 25 minutes, or until tomatoes are soft and tops are nicely browned.

Preparation time: 35 minutes

Blueberry Turnovers

1. Prepare frozen turnovers according to directions on the box. Serve with vanilla ice cream.

Cold Seafood Spread   Cheese & Crackers

Baked Chicken with Mushroom Sauce   Nutty Rice

Spinach-Artichoke Casserole   Radish Salad   Baked Apples

BLOCK PARTY

Every once in a while it's good to be neighborly. And it can be a lot of fun without tons of work. Here's how to be creative and not spend a lot of time or money, with a buffet in a relaxed setting. ♀ Serve red or white wine, if desired.

SHOPPING LIST

1 pound (450 g) prepared seafood
   salad (from deli)
5 whole boneless chicken breasts
1 red bell pepper
4 small (170 g) bags radishes
4 heads bibb lettuce
1 bunch red or green seedless
   grapes
10 large baking apples
1 lemon
1 bunch fresh parsley
2 pints (1 l) sour cream
4 ounces (115 g) cheddar cheese
   for grating
4 ounces (115 g) Swiss cheese
   for grating
2 ounces (60 g) Parmesan cheese
   for grating
1½-pound (750 g) wedge Gouda
   cheese
6 10-ounce (300 g) packages
   frozen chopped spinach
3 10¾-ounce (300 g) cans
   condensed cream of mushroom
   soup
2 3-ounce (85 g) cans whole
   mushrooms
1 6-ounce (170 g) jar marinated
   artichoke hearts
2 1-pound (450 g) boxes crackers
3 cups (650 ml) herb-flavored
   stuffing mix
1 pound (450 g) long-grain rice
1 4-ounce (115 g) package sliced
   almonds
1 bottle (750 ml) dry white wine

Staples
Vinaigrette or other basic salad
   dressing
Italian-seasoned bread crumbs
Granulated sugar
Curry powder
Ground cinnamon
Grated nutmeg

Cold Seafood Spread

1 pound (450 g) prepared
   seafood salad
1 to 2 teaspoons curry
   powder
1 1-pound (450 g) box
   crackers of your choice

1. Chop the salad to make a spread.

2. Add the curry to taste and refrigerate until ready to serve.

3. Place in a mound in the center of a serving plate and arrange crackers around.

Preparation time: 10 minutes
Requires advance preparation

Cheese and Crackers

1½-pound (750 g) wedge
   Gouda cheese
1 large bunch seedless
   grapes
1 1-pound (450 g) box
   crackers of your choice

Put the wedge of cheese on a serving plate. Snip the grapes into small sprigs and put alongside the cheese. Surround with crackers, and serve with a cheese knife for cutting individual portions.

Preparation time: 10 minutes

Baked Chicken with Mushroom Sauce

5 boneless and skinless
whole chicken breasts

4 tablespoons (60 ml)
vegetable oil

3 10¾-ounce (300 g) cans
condensed cream of
mushroom soup

1 pint (500 ml) sour cream

2 cups (500 ml) dry white
wine

2 3-ounce (85 g) cans whole
mushrooms

1 cup (125 g) grated Swiss
cheese

3 cups (300 g) herb-flavored
stuffing mix

1 cup (125 g) grated cheddar
cheese

Freshly ground black pepper

1. Preheat the oven to 350° F (180° C).

2. Cut the chicken breasts in half and remove any cartilage and fat. Heat 2 tablespoons oil in a large skillet and brown half the chicken breasts over medium heat for 4 minutes, turning occasionally. Remove chicken from pan, add remaining oil, and brown remaining chicken.

3. Mix soup, sour cream, wine, and mushrooms in a bowl.

4. Place the chicken in a greased baking dish and sprinkle on the Swiss cheese. Pour the soup mixture over. In another bowl, mix the stuffing and cheddar cheese, then spread over the top of the casserole. Sprinkle pepper on top.

5. Bake for 35 to 40 minutes, or until the top is lightly browned and crisp.

Preparation time: 1 hour

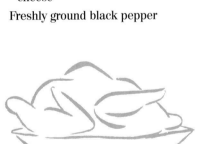

Nutty Rice

1 pound (450 g) long-grain
   white rice
1 red bell pepper
1 4-ounce (115 g) package
   sliced almonds
1 finely chopped red pepper

1. Follow the directions on the box
of rice to cook until tender.

2. Core and seed the red pepper,
then chop fine.

3. Add the almonds and red pepper
to the hot rice, and serve.

Preparation time: 20 minutes

Spinach-Artichoke Casserole

6 10-ounce (300 g) packages
   frozen chopped spinach
4 marinated artichoke hearts
   (1 6-ounce jar; 170 g)
1 pint (50 ml) sour cream
½ cup (65 g) grated
   Parmesan cheese
1 cup (100 g) bread crumbs

1. Preheat the oven to 350° F
(180° C). Cook the spinach according to package directions, then
drain well.

2. Cut the artichoke hearts into
small pieces.

3. Combine the spinach, artichokes,
sour cream, and cheese in a baking
dish and top with bread crumbs.

4. Bake for 30 minutes, or until
bubbly.

Preparation time: 45 minutes

Radish Salad

4 small (170 g) bags fresh
  radishes
4 heads bibb lettuce
1 cup (250 ml) vinaigrette
  dressing
1 cup (40 g) chopped
  fresh parsley
Freshly ground black pepper

1. Slice the radishes.

2. Place 2 or 3 lettuce leaves on each plate, then top with 10 to 12 radish slices. Drizzle on the dressing, and sprinkle with parsley and pepper.

Preparation time: 20 minutes

Baked Apples

10 large baking apples,
  such as Rome Beauty
2 teaspoons sugar
2 teaspoons ground
  cinnamon
2 teaspoons grated nutmeg
Juice of 1 small lemon

1. Preheat the oven to 350° F (180° C). Core the apples, but do not peel. Mix the sugar, cinnamon, and nutmeg in a small bowl, then use to stuff the apples.

2. Place the apples in a large baking dish and surround with 2 cups (500 ml) water. Sprinkle on the lemon juice, then bake for 30 minutes, or until apples are soft and centers are syrupy. Let cool briefly before serving.

Preparation time: 1 hour

Roasted Pecans   **Great Gazpacho**

Tropical Island Skewers   **Pasta with Lemon Butter**

Marinated Vegetables   **Pears in Red Wine**

DINNER WITH A VIEW

Have you ever invited someone to dinner but waited until the last minute to go to the grocery store? When you arrive at the store you turn into the vegetable aisle, and there is a good friend you haven't seen in over a year. Twenty minutes later, you throw anything that looks edible into your cart and head for the check-out. Stopping at the salad bar on the way gives you a big head start on the vegetable dish.

SHOPPING LIST

- ½ pound (225 g) scallops
- ½ pound (225 g) shrimp
- 4 ounces (115 g) green beans
- 8 baby carrots
- 10 whole mushrooms
- 1 cup (100 g) chopped broccoli from salad bar
- 1 cup (100 g) chopped cauliflower from salad bar
- 3 small garlic cloves
- 6 to 8 limes
- 1 bunch fresh dill
- 2 pears
- 1 small bunch parsley
- ½ pound (225 g) butter
- ½ pint (250 ml) sour cream
- 2 8-ounce (250 ml) cans seasoned vegetable juice
- ½ pound (225 g) fusilli or other pasta
- 1 4-ounce (115 g) bag shelled pecans
- 1 bottle (750 ml) dry red wine

Staples

- Tabasco sauce
- Red wine vinegar
- Olive oil
- Granulated sugar
- Salt and pepper
- 4 long wooden skewers

Roasted Pecans

1 cup (100 g) shelled pecans
½ cup (115 g) butter, melted
Salt

1. Preheat the oven to 400° F (200° C). Spread the pecans evenly on a cookie sheet. Drizzle melted butter over pecans, then season to taste with salt. Bake for 10 minutes, or until hot and glistening.

Preparation time: 15 minutes

Great Gazpacho

Left-over salad (undressed) from the night before
2 cups (500 ml) seasoned vegetable juice, such as V-8
3 dashes Tabasco sauce
1 small garlic clove, crushed
1 tablespoon (15 ml) red wine vinegar
1 pint (500 ml) sour cream

1. Place salad, vegetable juice, Tabasco, garlic, and vinegar in a blender. Blend until moderately smooth; leave it a little chunky.

2. Garnish with sour cream.

Preparation time: 10 minutes

Tropical Island Skewers

6 to 8 limes
½ cup (75 ml) olive oil
1 bunch fresh dill, chopped
Black pepper
2 garlic cloves, crushed
½ pound (225 g) scallops
½ pound (225 g) shrimp, shelled and deveined
4 wooden skewers

1. Squeeze the limes into a pan. Add the olive oil, dill, black pepper, and garlic to make a marinade.

2. Thread scallops and shrimp, alternately, on the skewers, and marinate in the lime mixture for about 1 hour.

3. Prepare a charcoal fire or pre-heat the broiler. Grill the skewers for 3 minutes on each side.

4. Heat marinade.

5. Serve scallops and shrimp over rice or pasta and pour marinade on top.

Preparation time: 1¼ hours

Pasta with Lemon Butter

½ pound (225 g) fusilli pasta
¼ cup (60 g) butter, melted
Juice of 1 small lemon
¼ cup (10 g) chopped fresh
  parsley

1. Cook the pasta according to package instructions.

2. Drain and rinse, then add butter, lemon juice, and parsley.

Preparation time: 25 minutes

Marinated Vegetables

4 ounces (115 g) green beans
10 whole fresh mushrooms
8 baby carrots
1 small zucchini
1 red bell pepper
1 small bunch asparagus
1 cup (100 g) chopped
  broccoli florets
1 cup (100 g) chopped
  cauliflower florets
½ cup (125 ml) vinaigrette
  dressing

1. Trim the beans and clean the mushrooms. Peel the baby carrots. Slice the zucchini and red pepper into thin strips. Snap rough ends off the asparagus and cut into bite-size pieces.

2. Blanch the vegetables, including the broccoli and cauliflower, in boiling water for 3 minutes. Arrange them in a design on a serving platter and sprinkle with dressing.

Preparation time: 45 minutes

Pears in Red Wine

2 Anjou or Bartlett pears
¾ cup (150 g) sugar
½ cup (125 ml) dry red wine
½ cup (125 ml) water

1. Peel the pears and cut in half lengthwise. Remove cores.

2. Bring the sugar, wine, and water to a boil in a saucepan and add pear halves. Cook until pears are soft, about 3 minutes. Remove from liquid and chill.

3. Continue to cook the poaching liquid until reduced and syrupy. Let cool, then spoon over the pears when serving.

Preparation time: 30 minutes
Requires advance preparation

dinner for twelve

Creamy Carrot Soup   Ham with a Mustard & Brown Sugar Glaze

Asparagus in Puff Pastry   Herbed Potatoes

Bakery Pie or Cake

A "MAD HATTER" EASTER

One year I made rabbit ears and whiskers out of felt, headbands, and pipe cleaners, and I required that everyone wear them at the dinner table. It certainly made for a very funny Easter. For this dinner, put a vase of daffodils on the table and scatter Easter candies around for a festive meal.

SHOPPING LIST

1 6- to 8-pound (2.8 to 3.6 kg)
  cooked ham
10 large carrots
2 pounds (900 g) thin asparagus
12 large potatoes
1 large onion
1 bunch fresh basil
1 bunch fresh dill
1 bunch fresh parsley
½ pint (250 ml) half-and-half
1 pint (500 ml) heavy cream
1 pound (450 g) thin-sliced Swiss
  cheese
4 ounces (125 g) Parmesan cheese
  for grating
1 quart (1 l) orange juice
2 1¼-pound (565 g) packages
  frozen puff pastry
2 10¾-ounce (300 g) cans chicken
  broth
1 8-ounce (250 ml) jar honey
  mustard
1 4-ounce (125 ml) jar honey
1 bottle (750 ml) dry white wine
1 8-ounce (250 ml) can beer
2 pies or 1 cake

Staples
Brown sugar
Dijon mustard
Unseasoned bread crumbs
Butter (½ stick; 60 g)
Salt and pepper

Creamy Carrot Soup

20 large carrots
2 large onions
½ cup (115 g) butter
8 cups (2 l) chicken broth
2 cups (500 ml) half-and-half
Salt and pepper

1. Peel and chop the carrots into 1-inch (2.5-cm) pieces. Chop the onion. Place with the butter in a large pot over medium heat. Sauté the onion for approximately 4 minutes, then add the broth. Bring to a boil. Add the carrots and cook until soft, approximately 15 minutes.

2. Put the mixture in a blender or food processor and blend until smooth. Add the half-and-half, mix thoroughly and season to taste, then serve.

Preparation time: 45 minutes

Ham with a Mustard and Brown Sugar Glaze

1 8-ounce (250 ml) jar
  honey mustard
1 cup (100 g) bread crumbs
1 cup (225 g) dark brown
  sugar
½ cup (75 ml) honey
2 cups (500 ml) orange juice
¼ cup (60 ml) beer
1 6- to 8-pound (2.8 to 3.6 kg)
  cooked ham

1. Preheat the oven to 325° F (170° C). Mix the mustard, bread crumbs, brown sugar, honey, ¼ cup (60 ml) orange juice, and beer in a bowl. Spread mixture over the ham and place in a baking dish. Pour remaining orange juice in the baking dish.

2. Roast for 1½ hours, basting 2 or 3 times during cooking.

Preparation time: 1¾ hours

Asparagus in Puff Pastry

2 pounds (900 g) thin
  asparagus
1 pound (450 g) thin-sliced
  Swiss cheese
¼ cup (60 ml) Dijon mustard
2 1¼-pound (565 g) packages
  frozen puff pastry

1. Preheat the oven to 400° F (200° C). Generously grease a large baking dish. Snap the rough ends off the asparagus, then steam for 3 minutes. Set aside to cool a bit.

2. Take 4 spears in your hand and wrap with a slice of Swiss cheese. Slather with mustard.

3. Unroll the pastry and cut into 2 × 3-inch (5 × 7.5 cm) pieces. Wrap a piece of puff pastry around the asparagus package and place asparagus in baking dish. Continue to make remaining "packages."

4. Bake for 15 minutes, or until crisp and flaky.

Preparation time: 45 minutes

Herbed Potatoes

12 large potatoes, sliced
1 pint (500 ml) heavy cream
1 cup (250 ml) dry white wine
¼ cup (10 g) chopped fresh
  basil
¼ cup (10 g) chopped fresh
  dill
¼ cup (10 g) chopped fresh
  parsley
1 cup (125 g) grated
  Parmesan cheese
Salt and pepper

1. Preheat the oven to 350° F (180° C). Generously grease a large baking dish.

2. Wash the potatoes, then slice thin and arrange in baking dish. Pour wine and cream over the potatoes, then sprinkle on the basil and dill. Cover the potatoes with Parmesan cheese, then season to taste with salt and pepper.

3. Bake for 45 minutes, or until potatoes are soft.

Preparation time: 1 hour

Tortellini Wrapped with Snow Peas   Pigs in a Blanket   Cucumber Canapes

Chicken à l'Orange   White & Wild Rice with Grapes & Rosemary   Cherry

Tomatoes Stuffed with Beans   Endive & Watercress Salad   Chocolate Ice Cream Pie

MOM'S 60TH

I don't know about your Mom, but mine raised nine children, and when she turned sixty, she certainly deserved an elegant tribute. It was a great occasion to bring together family and old friends. ❧ Special occasions deserve beautiful flowers. Sprinkle confetti on the table and hang streamers.

SHOPPING LIST

1 pound (450 g) hot dogs
8 whole skinless and boneless
   chicken breasts
1 pound (450 g) snow peas
2 large cucumbers
24 cherry tomatoes
1½ pounds (750 g) green beans
4 small heads Belgian endive
2 bunches watercress
1 bunch seedless red grapes
1 large red apple
1 bunch fresh dill
1 stick (115 g) butter
1 1-pound (450 g) package frozen
   cheese tortellini
1 10-ounce (300 g) can pizza crust
2 12-ounce (350 ml) cans frozen
   orange juice concentrate
½ gallon (2 l) chocolate chip ice
   cream
1 6-ounce (175 ml) jar honey
   mustard
1 8-ounce (250 ml) bottle chunky
   blue cheese dressing
1 8-ounce (250 ml) bottle
   chocolate sauce
2 1-ounce (30 g) envelopes dried
   onion soup mix
2 4-ounce (225 g) packages quick-
   cooking long-grain and wild rice
1 4-ounce (115 g) package shelled
   walnuts
1 commercial 9-inch (23-cm)
   chocolate cookie crust
1 bottle (750 ml) dry white wine
1 pint (500 ml) dark rum

Staples

Vinaigrette or other basic salad
   dressing
Dried dill
Dried rosemary

Tortellini Wrapped with Snow Peas

1 1-pound (450 g) bag frozen
   cheese tortellini
1 pound (450 g) snow peas
½ cup (125 ml) vinaigrette
   dressing

1. Cook the tortellini as instructed on package. Steam the snow peas for 3 to 5 minutes, so they will bend without breaking.

2. Wrap a pea around each tortellini and fasten with a toothpick. Place in a serving bowl.

3. Drizzle dressing over tortellini and let marinate until ready to serve.

Preparation time: 30 minutes

Pigs in a Blanket

1 pound (450 g) hot dogs
1 10-ounce (300 g) can frozen
   pizza crust
Honey mustard

1. Preheat the oven to 350° F (180° C). Lightly grease a large cookie sheet.

2. Unroll the pizza crust and cut into 2 × 3-inch (5 × 7.5 cm) rectangles. Spread with honey mustard, then roll each piece around a hot dog. Cut into ¾-inch (2 cm) pieces.

3. Place on cookie sheet and bake for 20 minutes, or until lightly browned.

Preparation time: 35 minutes

Cucumber Canapés

2 large cucumbers
½ cup (60 ml) chunky blue
   cheese dressing
Fresh dill sprigs

1. Score the sides of the cucumbers lengthwise with a fork and then slice about ⅛-inch (3 mm) thick.

2. Lay the slices on a dish. Spoon a little dressing on each and garnish with a sprig of dill.

3. Refrigerate until ready to serve.

Preparation time: 10 minutes

Chicken à l'Orange

2 1-ounce (30 g) envelopes
   dried onion soup mix
2 12-ounce (350 ml) cans
   frozen orange juice
   concentrate, thawed
½ cup (125 ml) dark rum
8 skinless and boneless
   whole chicken breasts

1. Preheat the oven to 350° F (180° C). Blend the soup mix with the orange juice concentrate and rum.

2. Trim the fat from the chicken and place in a large casserole. Pour the soup mixture over the chicken, cover the casserole with foil, and bake for 45 minutes, or until sauce is bubbly.

Preparation time: 55 minutes

White and Wild Rice with Grapes and Rosemary

2 4-ounce (115 g) boxes
  quick-cooking long-grain
  and wild rice
1 heaping tablespoon dried
  rosemary
1 cup (100 g) seedless red
  grapes, halved

1. Cook the wild rice according to the instructions on the box, adding the rosemary to the boiling water.

2. After the rice is cooked, add the grapes and keep warm until serving.

Preparation time: 20 minutes

Cherry Tomatoes Stuffed with Beans

24 cherry tomatoes
1½ pounds (750 g) green
  beans
1 tablespoon (15 g) butter

1 cup (250 ml) dry white wine
1 tablespoon dried dill

1. Preheat the oven to 300° F (150° C).

2. Cut the tops and bottoms off the cherry tomatoes and hollow out, making them into the shape of napkin rings.

3. Trim the string beans, then sauté in a frying pan with the butter for 5 minutes. Let cool.

4. Stuff the beans into the tomatoes so the ends are sticking out evenly on both sides.

5. Place in a baking dish with the wine and sprinkle dill over the top. Cover the baking dish with foil and bake for 5 minutes. Serve hot.

Preparation time: 25 minutes

Endive and Watercress Salad

4 Belgian endive
2 bunches watercress
1 cup (100 g) chopped apple
  (optional)
1 cup (100 g) walnuts
  (optional)
½ cup (125 ml) vinaigrette
  dressing

1. Cut about ½ inch (1 cm) off the root ends from the endive, separate the leaves, and rinse.

2. Rinse the watercress. Dry both greens thoroughly.

3. On each salad plate, arrange 4 or 5 endive leaves like a flower. Place 4 or 5 sprigs of watercress on top.

4. Sprinkle with chopped apple and walnuts.

5. Drizzle salad dressing on top and serve.

Preparation time: 15 minutes

Chocolate Ice Cream Pie

½ gallon (2 l) chocolate-chip
  ice cream
1 9-inch (23-cm) prepared
  chocolate cookie crust
Chocolate sauce

1. Soften ice cream briefly, then spread in the pie shell.

2. Freeze the pie until ice cream is hard again.

3. Drizzle each slice with some chocolate sauce when serving.

Preparation time: 10 minutes
Requires advance preparation

lunch for twelve

Asparagus Roll-ups   Crabmeat-Stuffed Chicken

Rice & Vegetable Medley   Mandarin Orange Salad

Herbed Pita Crisps   Fresh Melon with an Orange Dipping Sauce

THE BABY CHRISTENING

Some people may ask, "What does a single person know about baby christenings?" Well, as a proud godparent, who do you think was the ideal candidate to host the big lunch? You got it – me! For this event, decorate the center of the table with tiny wrapped baby gifts.

SHOPPING LIST

1 pound (450 g) prepared seafood salad (from deli)
6 skinless and boneless whole chicken breasts
5 heads bibb lettuce
1 Bermuda onion
2 yellow summer squash
2 large zucchini
1 bunch fresh parsley
1 lemon
1 large cantaloupe
1 small orange
½ pound (225 g) butter
3 8-ounce (675 g) packages cream cheese
1 pound (450 g) Parmesan cheese for grating
3 10-ounce (300 g) packages frozen asparagus
1 4-ounce (125 ml) container fresh orange juice
2 11-ounce (315 g) cans mandarin orange sections
1 8-ounce (250 ml) jar poppyseed dressing
1 1-pound (450 g) jar marshmallow cream
1 loaf thin-sliced white bread
8 pita breads
1 pound (450 g) quick-cooking white rice
1 bottle (750 ml) dry white wine

Staples
Mayonnaise
Dried dill
Dried rosemary
Curry powder
Black pepper

Asparagus Roll-ups

3 10-ounce (300 g) packages asparagus, thawed
½ cup (115 g) butter, melted
Thin slices of white bread
Juice of 1 lemon
1 cup (250 ml) mayonnaise
1 cup (125 g) grated Parmesan cheese

1. Preheat the oven to 350° F (180° C). Cut the crusts from the bread and roll flat.

2. Mix lemon juice with mayonnaise and spread on bread slices, then sprinkle on Parmesan cheese.

3. Place 1 stalk of asparagus on the end of one bread slice and roll up bread around stalk. Cut into 3 pieces and drizzle butter on top. Repeat for remaining pieces.

4. Place on a cookie sheet and bake for 10 to 12 minutes, or until lightly browned.

Preparation time: 30 minutes

Crabmeat-Stuffed Chicken

6 skinless and boneless chicken breasts
1 pound (450 g) seafood salad, chopped fine
2 8-ounce (225 g) packages cream cheese, softened to room temperature
1 cup (125 g) grated Parmesan cheese
2 cups (500 ml) dry white wine

1. Preheat the oven to 350° F (180° C). Cut the chicken breasts in half and pound thin. Set aside.

2. Knead together the seafood salad, cream cheese, and Parmesan cheese. Roll into 12 balls slightly larger than a golf ball.

3. Wrap each breast half around a ball and place seam side down in a large casserole dish. Add wine and bake for 25 minutes, or until chicken is cooked.

Preparation time: 45 minutes

Rice and Vegetable Medley

1 pound (450 g) quick-
  cooking white rice
2 large zucchini
2 large yellow squash
½ cup (125 ml) dry white wine
1 teaspoon dried dill

1. Follow instructions on box to cook rice.

2. Chop the zucchini and yellow squash into ½-inch (1-cm) pieces. Place in a frying pan, add wine, and cook for 3 to 4 minutes, stirring occasionally.

3. Mix rice with the zucchini and squash. Stir in dill and serve.

Preparation time: 15 minutes

Mandarin Orange Salad

5 heads bibb lettuce
2 11-ounce cans (312 g)
  mandarin orange sections
1 large Bermuda onion,
  chopped
¼ cup (10 g) coarsely
  chopped fresh parsley
¼ cup (60 ml) poppyseed
  dressing

1. Clean the lettuce and put into a bowl.

2. Drain the oranges and add to lettuce along with the onion.

3. Sprinkle on parsley, add dressing, and toss.

Preparation time: 10 minutes

Herbed Pita Crisps

8 pita breads
½ cup (115 g) butter, softened
¾ cup (90 g) grated
  Parmesan cheese
1 tablespoon dried dill
1 tablespoon dried rosemary
2 teaspoons curry powder
Black pepper

1. Preheat the broiler.

2. Split the pitas open with a knife. Spread butter on the open side of each pita. Sprinkle Parmesan cheese and a small amount of each seasoning on each. Cut into quarters.

3. Broil until lightly brown, about 2 minutes.

Preparation time: 10 minutes

Fresh Melon with an Orange Dipping Sauce

1 large cantaloupe
Marshmallow cream
1 8-ounce (225 g) package
  cream cheese
2 tablespoons orange juice
1 tablespoon grated
  orange rind

1. Peel the cantaloupe and cut flesh into ½ × ¾-inch (1-cm × 1.5 cm) strips.

2. Lightly heat the marshmallow cream, cream cheese, orange juice, and orange rind in a saucepan. Pour into a small bowl and arrange cantaloupe pieces around for dipping. Serve with toothpicks.

Preparation time: 15 minutes

Sliced Fresh Melon & Berries

Heart-Shaped Egg-in-a-Nest   Home Fries with Bacon

VALENTINE'S DAY

Who ever said you needed to wait until dinner to be romantic? I like to start first thing in the morning! There is nothing like a cozy breakfast in bed. Place a rose in a small bud vase and put it on the tray, and don't forget the newspaper. What a great way to begin the day!

SHOPPING LIST

4 ounces (115 g) bacon
2 large potatoes
1 bunch scallions
1 small cantaloupe
½ pint (150 g) raspberries
2 large eggs
1 thick-sliced loaf whole
   wheat bread

Staples
Salt and pepper
Butter

Sliced Fresh Melon and Berries

1 small cantaloupe
½ pint (150 g) raspberries

1. Slice the melon in half crosswise and scoop out the seeds.

2. Fill centers with berries.

3. Place each on a plate, and serve.

Preparation time: 5 minutes

Heart-Shaped Egg-in-a-Nest

1 tablespoon (15 g) butter
2 thick slices bread
2 large eggs

1. Toast the bread once lightly in the toaster, then cut into large heart shapes and cut a round hole in the center of each.

2. Melt the butter in a large frying pan.

3. Place hearts in the butter, then break an egg into each center and cook until whites are firm, about 3 minutes. Serve at once.

Preparation time: 15 minutes

Home Fries with Bacon

4 slices bacon
2 baking potatoes
2 scallions (white parts only)
Salt and pepper

1. Cook the bacon in the frying pan and set aside. Keep bacon fat in the pan.

2. Cut up the potatoes into small cubes. Slice the scallions.

3. Put the potatoes and scallions in the bacon fat, then cook over medium heat for 15 to 20 minutes, or until potatoes are soft. Turn frequently.

4. Season to taste with salt and pepper.

Preparation time: 35 minutes

a meal for twelve friends

Bibb & Grapefruit Salad   Best Brunch Casserole

Cheese & Herb Muffins   Lemon Squares

NEW YEAR'S DAY BRUNCH

After a late night ringing in the New Year, there's nothing better than waking up to a mouth-watering feast, especially one prepared the day before but cooked fresh that morning (or afternoon). ⚲ Place a silver bowl of aspirin on the table for decor and for guests with hangovers. Use leftover party decorations from the night before – such as hats, blowers, and some streamers – to liven up the table.

SHOPPING LIST

½ pound (225 g) sliced bacon
2 ripe tomatoes
4 heads bibb lettuce
2 large grapefruit
1 bunch fresh parsley
1 quart (1 l) milk
1 dozen large eggs
1 8-ounce (225 g) package
   shredded cheddar cheese
4 ounces (125 g) Parmesan cheese
   for grating
2 3-ounce (85 g) cans sliced
   mushrooms
1 8-ounce (250 ml) bottle
   poppyseed dressing
1 large loaf French bread
12 English muffins
1 ounce dried rosemary
12 Lemon Squares

Staples
Pepper

Bibb and Grapefruit Salad

4 heads bibb lettuce, washed
2 large grapefruit, peeled and
   sectioned
¼ cup (10 g) chopped fresh
   parsley
½ cup (125 ml) poppyseed
   dressing

1. Place the lettuce leaves in a large bowl.

2. Add the grapefruit sections and parsley.

3. Add dressing and toss.

Preparation time: 15 minutes

Best Brunch Casserole

12 large eggs
1 8-ounce (225 g) package
   shredded cheddar cheese
1 loaf French bread, cut into
   ½-inch (1-cm) cubes
2 cups (500 ml) milk
2 ripe tomatoes, chopped
2 3-ounce (85 g) cans sliced
   mushrooms
½ pound (225 g) bacon,
   cooked and crumbled
Salt and pepper

1. Preheat the oven to 350° F (180° C).

2. Grease a large casserole dish. Line the bottom with half the bread cubes.

3. Beat together the eggs and milk, then pour half the mixture over the bread in the casserole. Sprinkle on half the cheese, tomatoes, mushrooms, and bacon.

4. Repeat with the remaining eggs and milk mixture, then the bread, cheese, tomatoes, and bacon.

4. Bake for 40 minutes, or until firm.

Preparation time: 1 hour

Cheese and Herb Muffins

12 English muffins, split
  in half
1 cup (125 g) grated
  Parmesan cheese
4 tablespoons dried
  rosemary
Freshly ground black pepper

1. Preheat the broiler.

2. Place the muffins on a cookie sheet and spread with butter.

3. Sprinkle a little cheese, rosemary, and pepper on each muffin.

4. Broil until light brown, about 3 minutes. Serve in a basket.

Preparation time: 15 minutes

Lemon Squares

1. Place purchased lemon squares on a plate and serve.

Potato Soup with Chives   Oriental Pork Loin

Sesame Noodles   Asparagus Steamed in Wine

Mixed Green Salad   Cookies & Cream Outrage

CHRISTMAS EVE HOMECOMING

Coming from a large New England family, I feel the holidays bring everyone close together. My favorite time is Christmas eve, when we are first all together and recall past holidays. ❧ For this meal, scatter Christmas balls and tinsel on the table for a decoration. And fill a basket with pine cones and holly for a centerpiece.

SHOPPING LIST

1 5-pound (2.2 kg) pork loin
6 large potatoes
1 medium onion
2 garlic cloves
3 pounds (1.4 kg) fresh asparagus
1 head romaine lettuce
1 head bibb lettuce
1 small head radicchio
1 bunch fresh chives
1 pint (300 g) raspberries
½ pint (250 ml) light cream
1 7-ounce (250 ml) container
   whipped cream
1 46-ounce (1.5 l) can chicken broth
1 8-ounce (230 g) jar orange
   marmalade
1 10-ounce (300 ml) bottle teriyaki
   marinade
1 1-ounce (30 g) box sesame seeds
1 pound (450 g) fusilli pasta
1 1-pound (450 g) package
   chocolate wafers
1 bottle (750 ml) dry white wine

Staples
Oriental sesame oil
Vinaigrette or other basic
   dressing
Butter (5 tablespoons; 75 g)
Salt and pepper

Potato Soup with Chives

2 tablespoons (30 g) butter
1 medium onion
1 46-ounce (1.5 l) can
   chicken broth
6 medium-large potatoes
1 cup (250 ml) light cream
Salt and pepper
½ cup (20 g) chopped
   fresh chives

1. Melt the butter in a fairly large pot over medium-high heat.

2. Chop the onion and add to the pot, stirring for 3 to 4 minutes.

3. Add the chicken broth and bring to a boil.

4. Peel and dice the potatoes into ½-inch (1-cm) cubes, then add to the broth. Cook for 10 to 12 minutes, or until potatoes are soft.

5. Put into a blender and blend until smooth. Add cream and salt and pepper to taste.

6. Garnish with chives, and serve hot or cold.

Preparation time: 45 minutes

Oriental Pork Loin

1 10-ounce (300 ml) bottle
   teriyaki marinade
1 8-ounce (230 g) jar orange
   marmalade
2 large garlic cloves, crushed
3 tablespoons sesame seeds
1 5-pound (2.2 kg) pork loin

1. Mix the marinade, marmalade, and garlic in a bowl. Pour over the pork and marinate at least several hours.

2. Preheat the oven to 375° F (190° C).

3. Remove meat from marinade and sprinkle with the sesame seeds. Bake for 1½ hours, or until roast is crisp on top and white in center.

4. Heat the leftover marinade on top of the stove for 5 to 10 minutes, and use as a sauce.

Preparation time: 2 hours
Requires advance preparation

Sesame Noodles

1 pound (450 g) fusilli
¼ cup (60 ml) oriental
  sesame oil
2 tablespoons sesame seeds
Salt and pepper

1. Bring salted water to a boil and cook pasta until al dente, about 10 minutes.

2. Drain and toss with sesame oil and sesame seeds. Season to taste with salt and pepper.

Preparation time: 25 minutes

Asparagus Steamed in Wine

3 pounds (1.4 kg) fresh
  asparagus
½ cup (125 ml) dry white wine
3 tablespoons (45 g) butter

1. Break rough ends off the asparagus, then place in a large frying pan over medium heat.

2. Add the wine and butter, cover, and steam for 8 to 10 minutes, or until tender-crisp.

Preparation time: 20 minutes

Mixed Green Salad

1 head romaine lettuce
1 head bibb lettuce
1 head red leaf lettuce
1 small head radicchio
Vinaigrette dressing

1. Wash and dry the lettuces and toss in a large salad bowl.

2. Mix in the radicchio and toss with dressing just before serving.

Preparation time: 15 minutes

Cookies and Cream Outrage

1 1-pound (450 g) package
  thin chocolate wafers
1 7-ounce (200 g) container
  whipped cream
1 pint (300 g) raspberries

1. Alternating wafers and whipped cream, make several rows to create four 6-inch logs.

2. Press each log together, then place logs in freezer until firm.

3. When ready to serve, slice lengthwise through each section.

4. Place a half on each plate and sprinkle raspberries on top.

Preparation time: 15 minutes
Requires advance preparation

Easy Havarti Cheese Spread   Broiled Shrimp

Caesar Salad   Herbed French Bread   Brownies

THE PAINTING PARTY

When you are on a tight budget but the dining room desperately needs a paint job, call on some friends – invite them for dinner, and tell them to dress **very** casually. ⚱ Use a dropcloth or newspaper as a tablecloth. Buy a bunch of flowers to put on the table; the contrast is great! ⚱ Serve a dry white wine with dinner. And place a brownie in a wine glass, topped with ice cream or whipped topping, for dessert.

SHOPPING LIST

2 pounds (900 g) large shrimp
2 heads romaine lettuce
1 garlic clove
1 lemon
1 bunch fresh dill
¾ pound (345 g) butter
1 pound (450 g) Havarti cheese
12 ounces (350 g) Parmesan cheese
1 8-ounce (250 ml) bottle Caesar
    salad dressing
1 loaf French bread
1 14-ounce (400 g) package
    croutons
Brownie mix

Staples
Mayonnaise
Dijon mustard
Pepper

Easy Havarti Cheese Spread

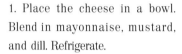

3 cups (450 g) shredded
    Havarti cheese
¼ cup (60 ml) mayonnaise
1 tablespoon Dijon mustard
¼ cup (10 g) chopped
    fresh dill

1. Place the cheese in a bowl. Blend in mayonnaise, mustard, and dill. Refrigerate.

2. An hour before serving, remove from the refrigerator and let it warm up slightly.

3. Serve at room temperature with crackers.

Preparation time: 10 minutes
Requires advance preparation

Broiled Shrimp

2 pounds (900 g) large
    shrimp
1 cup (230 g) butter, melted
1 lemon
2 teaspoons minced garlic
Cracked pepper

1. Preheat the broiler.

2. Place the shrimp on an edged cookie sheet and pour melted butter on top. Squeeze the lemon all over the shrimp and sprinkle with garlic and pepper.

3. Broil for 2 to 3 minutes, or until shrimp is opaque. Serve with French bread and salad.

Preparation time: 15 minutes

Caesar Salad

2 heads romaine lettuce, washed

1 14-ounce (400 g) package prepared croutons

1 8-ounce (250 ml) bottle Caesar salad dressing

½ cup (65 g) freshly grated Parmesan cheese

Freshly ground pepper

1. Trim the lettuce and tear leaves. Place on salad plates or in a salad bowl.

2. Add the croutons and toss with dressing.

3. Sprinkle Parmesan cheese on top, and season to taste with pepper.

Preparation time: 20 minutes

Herbed French Bread

1 loaf French bread

½ cup (115 g) butter

2 tablespoons chopped dill

2 tablespoons (15 g) grated Parmesan cheese

1. Preheat the oven to 350° F (180° F. Cut the bread lengthwise down the middle.

2. Place small pats of butter every few inches, then sprinkle with dill and cheese.

3. Put halves together again and wrap in foil.

4. Bake for 15 minutes, or until butter has melted.

Preparation time: 30 minutes

Brownies

1 box brownie mix

1. Prepare brownies according to package instructions.

Preparation time: 40 minutes

Zucchini Soup   Fettuccine with Shrimp

Garden Salad   Sliced Oranges with Grand Marnier

"SPRING FEVER"

Winter is finally behind us and the daffodils are out in force. The weather is beautiful, the breezes are warm. What a perfect day for a walk in the country and a late lunch outdoors in the sun. A bunch of spring flowers set in a pitcher is nice as a centerpiece. Fresh iced tea or lemonade is also a springtime tradition.

SHOPPING LIST

1½ pounds (750 g) shrimp
1 pound (450 g) zucchini
1 small onion
1 garlic clove
2 large tomatoes
1 medium cucumber
1 medium carrot
1 small (170 g) bag radishes
1 large head lettuce
4 large oranges
1 bunch fresh parsley
1 bunch watercress
½ pint (250 ml) half-and-half
1 8-ounce (250 ml) container
   frozen Alfredo sauce
1 10¾-ounce (300 g) can
   chicken broth
1 pound (450 g) fettuccine
Grand Marnier

Staples

Curry powder
Salad dressing
Butter (½ stick; 60 g)
Salt and pepper

Zucchini Soup

2 tablespoons (30 g) butter
1 small onion, chopped
1 pound (450 g) zucchini,
   sliced
1 small bunch watercress,
   trimmed with only 1 inch
   (2.5 cm) of stem
2 cups (500 ml) chicken broth
½ cup (125 ml) half-and-half
1 teaspoon curry powder
Salt and pepper

1. Put the butter, onion, zucchini, watercress, and broth in a large pot and cook over medium-high heat for 10 to 15 minutes, or until vegetables are tender.

2. Pour into a blender and blend until smooth.

3. Add the half-and-half, curry powder, and salt and pepper to taste.

4. Serve hot or cold.

Preparation time: 30–45 minutes

Fettuccine with Shrimp

1 pound (450 g) fettuccine
2 tablespoons (30 g) butter
1 garlic clove, crushed
1½ pounds (750 g) shrimp,
   peeled and deveined
1 8-ounce (250 ml) container
   frozen Alfredo sauce,
   thawed
½ cup (125 ml) white wine
   (optional)
¼ cup (10 g) chopped
   fresh parsley

1. Cook the pasta in boiling salted water until al dente, about 5 minutes. Drain and keep warm.

2. Heat the butter in a large skillet and add the garlic and shrimp. Sauté until shrimp are opaque, about 5 minutes.

3. Pour the sauce over the shrimp and heat through.

4. Pour the shrimp sauce over the pasta, add the wine, and sprinkle with parsley.

Preparation time: 30 minutes

Garden Salad

2 large tomatoes, sliced

1 medium cucumber, sliced

1 medium carrot, julienned

1 small (170 g) bag radishes, sliced

1 large head lettuce, washed

Dressing of choice

1. Mix vegetables with lettuce in a big bowl.

2. Toss with dressing.

Preparation time: 15 minutes

Sliced Oranges with Grand Marnier

4 medium navel oranges

3 ounces (6 tablespoons; 90 ml) Grand Marnier

1. Slice the oranges and cut off the skin.

2. Place 3 to 4 slices on each plate and pour 1 tablespoon Grand Marnier over each serving.

Preparation time: 15 minutes

Quick Pâté   Sweet Potato Soup   Apricot-Glazed Game Hens

with Wild Rice Stuffing   Creamed Onions   Minted Baby Peas

Apple Crisp with Ice Cream

A QUIET THANKSGIVING

When work is hectic and the Thanksgiving holiday isn't quite long enough for a plane ride to see relatives, it can be refreshing to prepare an elegant dinner for two. Beaujolais Nouveau comes out around Thanksgiving, so think of serving it with this meal. Buy a small plant for the table centerpiece.

SHOPPING LIST

1 pound (450 g) chicken livers
4 slices bacon
2 game hens
2 small onions
4 medium sweet potatoes
1 green apple
1 red apple
4 Rome Beauty or other cooking
   apples
1 small bunch red seedless grapes
1 small bunch green seedless
   grapes
1 bunch fresh mint
1 bunch fresh parsley
1 pound (450 g) butter
2 pints (1 l) heavy cream
1 ounce (30 g) blue cheese
1 ounce (30 g) Swiss cheese for
   grating
1 ounce (30 g) Parmesan cheese
   for grating
1 10-ounce (300 g) package frozen
   tiny peas
1 pint (500 ml) vanilla ice cream
2 10¾-ounce (300 ml) cans chicken
   broth
2 15-ounce (425 g) jars baby onions
1 8-ounce (230 g) jar apricot
   preserves
1 3-ounce (85 g) can sliced
   mushrooms
1 4-ounce (115 g) package pecans
1 1-ounce (30 g) envelope dried
   onion soup mix
1 cup (200 g) wild rice
1 bottle (750 ml) dry white wine
1 pint (500 ml) dark rum

Staples
Mayonnaise
Flour
Brown sugar

Quick Pâté

4 slices bacon
1 small onion, chopped
1 pound (450 g) chicken livers
1 ounce (2 tablespoons;
   15 ml) dark rum
½ cup (125 ml) mayonnaise

1. Cook the bacon until crisp in a frying pan with the onion.

2. Add the chicken livers and rum, and sauté over medium heat until cooked, about ten minutes.

3. Place the livers and mayonnaise in a food processor or blender and blend until smooth.

4. Serve at room temperature with crackers.

Preparation time: 25 minutes

Sweet Potato Soup

4 medium sweet potatoes
1 small onion
2 tablespoons (30 g) butter
2 10¾-ounce (300 g) cans
   chicken broth
1 pint (500 ml) heavy cream
¼ cup (25 g) chopped pecans
¼ cup (30 g) crumbled
   blue cheese

1. Peel and dice the potatoes. Chop the onion.

2. Melt the butter in a large pot, add the onion, and cook, stirring continually, for 3 to 4 minutes, or until translucent.

3. Add the chicken broth and potatoes and boil for 10 to 12 minutes or until soft.

4. Pour into a blender and blend until smooth. Add the cream, then pour soup into bowls, keeping hot.

5. Sprinkle the pecans and cheese on top and serve.

Preparation time: 30 minutes

Apricot-Glazed Game Hens with Wild Rice Stuffing

1 cup (200 g) wild rice

1 8-ounce (230 g) jar apricot preserves

1 1-ounce (30 g) envelope dried onion soup mix

2 game hens

1 red and 1 green apple, cored and chopped

1 small bunch each red and green seedless grapes, chopped

2 ounces (4 tablespoons; 60 ml) dark rum

¼ cup (10 g) chopped fresh parsley

1 3-ounce (85 g) can sliced mushrooms

1. Cook the wild rice in boiling salted water for 45 minutes. Preheat the oven to 350° F (180° C).

2. Mix the marmalade and onion soup in a bowl and slather all over the outside of the hens.

3. Combine the rice with the fruit and parsley, and stir in the rum and mushrooms.

4. Stuff the hens with the rice mixture, secure with picks, and place in the baking pan for 40 minutes, or until juices run clear.

Preparation time: 2 hours

Creamed Onions

4 tablespoons (60 g) butter

2 tablespoons (18 g) all-purpose flour

1 pint (500 ml) heavy cream

¼ cup (30 g) shredded Swiss cheese

¼ cup (30 g) grated Parmesan cheese

¼ cup (60 ml) dry white wine

2 15-ounce (425 g) jars baby onions, drained

1. Melt the butter and slowly add the flour, making a paste. Cook for 1 minute, then add the cream and the cheeses.

2. Stir in the wine, then add the onions and simmer for 15 to 20 minutes over low heat.

Preparation time: 30 minutes

Minted Baby Peas

1 10-ounce (300 g) package frozen tiny peas

½ cup (125 ml) dry white wine

2 tablespoons chopped fresh mint

1 tablespoon (15 g) butter

1. Gently heat the peas in a pan with the wine, mint, and butter. Cook over medium heat for about 5 minutes.

Preparation time: 10 minutes

Apple Crisp with Ice Cream

4 Rome Beauty apples

2 tablespoons (18 g) all-purpose flour

4 tablespoons (50 g) brown sugar

½ cup (115 g) butter, melted

1 pint (500 ml) vanilla ice cream

1. Preheat the oven to 325° F (180° C).

2. Peel, core, and slice the apples crosswise into rings. Place the apples in a greased baking dish.

3. Gradually stir the flour and brown sugar into the butter, then sprinkle the mixture over the apples.

4. Bake for 30 minutes, or until bubbly. Serve with vanilla ice cream.

Preparation time: 45 minutes

Baked Brie   Breaded Chicken Breasts   Wild Rice with Walnuts

Carrots Steamed in Grapefruit Juice   Tortellini Salad

Rum-Baked Bananas

"I FINALLY GOT UP THE NERVE"

Have you ever met someone at a party or some other social event and the spark was there? Then you bump into that person at a few other functions? Well, you won't know if you don't ask!

SHOPPING LIST

2 skinless and boneless whole
  chicken breasts
4 large carrots
1 medium tomato
1 head romaine lettuce
1 green apple
1 lemon
1 large banana
1 bunch fresh parsley
1 bunch fresh dill
1 4½-ounce (130 g) brie
1 pint (500 ml) vanilla ice cream
1 10-ounce (300 g) package frozen
  long-grain and wild rice
1 10-ounce (300 g) can frozen
  pizza crust
2 ounces (60 g) shelled walnuts
1 1-pound (450 g) package cheese
  tortellini
1 pint (500 ml) dark rum

Staples
Honey mustard
Vinaigrette
Italian-seasoned bread crumbs
Pepper

Baked Brie

1 10-ounce (300 g) can frozen
  pizza crust
1 4½-ounce (130 g) brie,
  chilled
Honey mustard
1 green apple, sliced

1. Preheat the oven to 425° F
(220° C).

2. Take the dough out of the can
and unroll it on a flat surface. Cut
into 6-inch (15 cm) squares.

3. Cut the brie into 2 half-moons
and slather honey mustard on top
of each. Wrap each half with a
square of pizza dough, making sure
that none of the cheese is exposed.

4. Place the brie on a greased baking dish, and bake for 12 minutes,
or until dough is lightly browned.
Serve with sliced apple.

Preparation time: 20 minutes

Breaded Chicken Breasts

2 skinless and boneless
  chicken breasts
Vinaigrette dressing
1 cup (100 g) Italian-
  seasoned bread crumbs
Pepper

1. Preheat the oven to 425° F
(220° C).

2. Cut the chicken breasts in half,
remove any fat, and rinse.

3. Place the dressing in a bowl and
the bread crumbs on a plate. Dip
the chicken in the dressing and roll
in the bread crumbs. Place the
chicken in a greased baking dish
and sprinkle with pepper.

4. Bake for 15 minutes, or until chicken is cooked through
and crisp.

Preparation time: 25 minutes

Wild Rice with Walnuts

1 10-ounce (300 g) package
  frozen long-grain and
  wild rice
½ cup (50 g) chopped walnuts
2 teaspoons grated lemon
  rind
½ cup (20 g) chopped
  fresh parsley

1. Cook the rice according to package directions. Add the walnuts, lemon rind, and parsley, and stir well.

Preparation time: 20 minutes

Carrots Steamed in Grapefruit Juice

4 large carrots
1¼ cups (350 ml) grapefruit
  juice
1 tablespoon chopped
  fresh dill

1. Peel and cut the carrots into 2-inch strips ¼-inch (½ cm) wide.

2. Boil in the grapefruit juice for 10 minutes, or until tender. Garnish with dill.

Preparation time: 20 minutes

Tortellini Salad

1 1-pound (450 g) package
  cheese tortellini
1 head romaine lettuce,
  washed
1 ripe tomato
2 tablespoons chopped
  fresh parsley
Vinaigrette dressing

1. Follow directions on package for cooking tortellini and set aside.

2. Tear the lettuce into bite-size pieces. Arrange on salad plates or in bowls.

3. Cut the tomato into quarters and place on lettuce with tortellini in middle. Sprinkle with parsley and drizzle with dressing.

Preparation time: 20 minutes

Rum-Baked Bananas

1 ripe banana
2 ounces (4 tablespoons;
  60 ml) dark rum
Vanilla ice cream

1. Preheat the oven to 400° F (200° C).

2. Peel and cut the banana lengthwise and place face up in a baking dish. Pour rum over each half and cover dish tightly with foil.

3. Bake for 20 minutes. Serve with vanilla ice cream.

Preparation time: 30 minutes

Winter Squash Soup   Bright Pepper Salad

Broiled New Potatoes   Stuffed Beef Tenderloin

Poached Pears with Chocolate Sauce

"ONLY THE BEST FOR THE BOSS"

You have been invited to the boss's house three times and you have had two promotions. You have been working there for three years, and you are beginning to feel a bit awkward and guilty. Don't you think it's time?

SHOPPING LIST

1 5-pound (2.2 kg) beef tenderloin
6 Anjou or Bartlett pears
1 bunch fresh mint
1 ounce (30 g) Parmesan cheese
   for grating
4 ounces (125 g) cheddar cheese
   for grating
4 ounces (125 g) Swiss cheese
   for grating
2 10-ounce (300 g) packages
   frozen winter squash
2 10-ounce (300 g) packages
   frozen spinach
2 6-ounce (170 g) jars marinated
   artichoke hearts
2 10¾-ounce (300 g) cans
   chicken broth
1 pint (500 ml) apple cider
1 16-ounce (500 ml) can
   chocolate syrup
1 fifth (750 ml) medium-dry sherry
1 bottle (750 ml) dry red wine

Staples
Dried rosemary
Ground cinnamon
Vinaigrette
Mustard
Salt and pepper

Winter Squash Soup

2 10¾-ounce (300 g) cans
   chicken broth
2 10-ounce (300 g) packages
   frozen winter squash,
   thawed
1 teaspoon dried rosemary
¼ cup (60 ml) medium-dry
   sherry

1. Put the chicken broth into a large pot.

2. Add the squash and rosemary, and bring to a boil.

3. Simmer and stir until thoroughly blended.

4. Add the sherry and keep warm until serving.

Preparation time: 15 minutes

Bright Pepper Salad

1 yellow bell pepper
1 red bell pepper
1 green bell pepper
½ cup (125 ml) vinaigrette
   dressing
2 tablespoons chopped
   fresh mint

1. Cut the peppers into ¼-inch (½-cm) strips, then place in a bowl.

2. Add the mint and dressing. Mix and let sit until serving time.

Preparation time: 15 minutes

Broiled New Potatoes

10 new potatoes
¼ cup (30 g) grated
   Parmesan cheese
1 cup (125 g) grated cheddar
   cheese
1 cup (125 g) grated Swiss
   cheese
4 heaping teaspoons grainy
   mustard
Salt and pepper

1. Cook the potatoes in boiling water for 30 minutes. Drain and cut each in half, then cut a small slice off the ends. Place on a cookie sheet.

1. Preheat the broiler. In a separate bowl, mix the cheeses and mustard.

3. Using a teaspoon, scoop out a small amount of potato from each round, almost creating a bowl, and fill with the cheese mixture.

4. Broil until bubbly and brown.

Preparation time: 1 hour

Stuffed Beef Tenderloin

2 10-ounce (300 g) packages
   frozen chopped spinach,
   thawed
2 6-ounce (170 g) jars
   marinated artichoke hearts
1 box herbed cheese
Salt and pepper
1 5-pound (2.2 kg) trimmed
   beef tenderloin
1 cup (250 ml) dry red wine

1. Preheat the oven to 450° F (230° C).

2. Drain the spinach and place in a medium bowl. Drain the liquid from the artichoke jars and add to the spinach. Stir in the cheese and generous amounts of pepper. Mix well.

3. Place the tenderloin in a broiling or baking pan. With a sharp knife, cut an incision lengthwise, making a pocket; do not cut through the ends. Place the stuffing mixture inside the pocket, filling it as full as you can. Close with skewers.

4. Set aside any leftover stuffing mixture; you can bake it separately and serve it with the rest of the meal.

5. Pour the red wine into the pan and sprinkle meat with salt and pepper. Bake for 20 to 30 minutes for rare, longer for better done.

Preparation time: 45 minutes

Poached Pears with Chocolate Sauce

2 cups (500 ml) apple cider
6 Anjou or Bartlett pears
Ground cinnamon
¾ cup (175 ml) chocolate
   syrup

1. Place the cider in a large pot and bring to a boil.

2. Peel the pears and place them in the boiling cider. Sprinkle with cinnamon, cover pot, and simmer for 5 minutes, or until pears are soft.

3. Drain and place 1 pear in a dessert bowl. Reduce the cooking liquid over high heat until syrupy.

4. Pour the syrup over and around the pears, then drizzle two tablespoons of chocolate syrup over each pear before serving.

Preparation time: 20 minutes

Cream Cheese Dip & Chips   Bachelor's Seafood Casserole

Sliced Tomatoes with Dill   French Bread

Ice Cream & Raspberries

SUNDAY EVENING AFTER THE GAME

I have always liked to entertain on Sunday evenings because it seems to make the weekend just that much longer – like a three-day weekend.

SHOPPING LIST

4 large fillets of sole or flounder,
about 1½ (750 g) pounds total
4 large tomatoes
1 pint (300 g) raspberries
1 bunch fresh dill
1 8-ounce (225 g) package cream
cheese
1 pint (500 ml) mint chocolate chip
ice cream
3 10-ounce (900 g) packages
frozen chopped spinach
1 6-ounce (160 g) can tiny shrimp
2 10¾-ounce (300 g) cans lobster
bisque or cream of shrimp soup
1 6-ounce (175 g) jar mango
chutney
1 12-ounce (350 g) package corn
chips
1 bottle (750 ml) medium-dry
sherry
½ pound (225 g) French cookies
(from bakery)

Staples

Vinaigrette or other basic salad
dressing
Curry powder

Cream Cheese Dip and Chips

1 8-ounce (225 g) package
cream cheese
½ teaspoon curry powder
3 heaping tablespoons
mango chutney
Corn chips

1. Place the cream cheese in a pot
over medium heat.

2. As it begins to soften, add the
chutney and curry powder.

3. Stir until well mixed, then pour
into a small bowl.

4. Surround with chips.

Preparation time: 10 minutes

Bachelor's Seafood Casserole

3 10-ounce (300 g) packages
frozen chopped spinach,
thawed
4 large fillets of sole or
flounder, about 1½ pounds
(750 g) total
1 6-ounce (160 g) can tiny
shrimp
2 10¾-ounce (300 g) cans
lobster bisque or cream of
shrimp soup
½ cup (125 ml) medium-dry
sherry

1. Preheat the oven to 350° F
(180° C).

2. Generously grease a 9 × 12-inch
(23 × 30-cm) baking dish.

3. Drain the spinach well, then
place in the baking dish, spreading evenly. Place fish fillets over
the spinach and sprinkle with
the shrimp.

4. In a medium bowl, mix the
soup and sherry, then pour over
the fish. Bake for 35 minutes, or
until fish flakes.

Preparation time: 1 hour

Sliced Tomatoes
with Dill

4 ripe large tomatoes
Vinaigrette dressing
2 tablespoons chopped
  fresh dill

1. Slice the tomatoes and arrange in a circle on a plate.

2. Pour the dressing over and sprinkle with dill.

Preparation time: 10 minutes

Ice Cream
with Raspberries

1 pint (500 ml) mint
  chocolate chip ice cream
1 pint (300 g) fresh
  raspberries
½ pound (225 g) bakery
  French cookies

1. Scoop the ice cream into wine glasses and spoon some fresh raspberries on top of each serving.

2. Place the glasses on small saucers, and serve with a cookie or two.

Preparation time: 10 minutes

Tomato Soup   Avocado Salad

Bermuda's Best   Apples

"WHAT A SURPRISE!"

In our hectic world, when you and your significant other feel like two ships passing in the night, it's nice to be spontaneous. A little effort goes a long way. Here's an easy and delicious office meal to perk up both your days.

¾ pound (350 g) sliced roast beef
1 Bermuda onion
2 ripe avocados
3 ripe tomatoes
2 red apples
1 quart (1 l) milk
1 4-ounce (115 g) package Boursin
  cheese
2 10¾-ounce (300 g) cans tomato
  soup
1 14-ounce (400 g) package soft
  flour tortillas
1 bottle (750 ml) medium-dry
  sherry

Staples
Dried dill
Vinaigrette or other basic
  salad dressing
Dijon mustard
Mayonnaise

Tomato Soup

2 10¾-ounce (300 g) cans
  tomato soup
2 soup-cans of milk
1 ripe tomato, chopped
1 teaspoon dried dill
¼ cup (60 ml) medium-dry
  sherry

1. Follow directions on can for pre-paring tomato soup made with milk.

2. Add the tomato, dill, and sherry. Stir well, then place in thermos to keep warm.

Preparation time: 10 minutes

Avocado Salad

2 ripe avocados
2 ripe tomatoes, cut in
   ½-inch (1-cm) cubes
1 tablespoon Dijon mustard
¼ cup (60 ml) vinaigrette
   dressing

1. Cut the avocados in half, re-moving the skin. Remove the pit and cut flesh into ¼-inch (½-cm) pieces.

2. Place avocados and tomatoes in a bowl. Mix mustard and salad dressing and pour on top.

Preparation time: 10 minutes

Bermuda's Best

1 4-ounce (115 g) package
   herbed cheese
½ cup (120 ml) mayonnaise
4 flour tortillas
1 Bermuda onion, chopped
¾ pound (350 g) sliced
   roast beef

1. Mix the cheese and mayon-naise, then slather on one side of each tortilla.

2. Sprinkle the onion on the tor-tillas and place some roast beef over that. Roll and cut in half, plac-ing a toothpick through each roll.

Preparation time: 15 minutes

easy dinner for thirty

Tomato & Mozzarella Salad   Pasta Salad

Barbecued Chicken   Corn Muffins

Watermelon & Brownies

"THE PAYBACK"

It can start to be embarrassing when you have been invited to friends' houses but have never returned the favor. After about six to eight months, you'll find you owe a lot of people. My suggestion is to get it all over at once. The more the merrier!

60 pieces of chicken (wings, thighs, legs), about 15 pounds (6.75 kg)
2 medium zucchini
2 medium yellow squash
1 bunch broccoli
12 cherry tomatoes
10 large tomatoes
12 large mushrooms
2 yellow bell peppers
2 red bell peppers
1 large watermelon
1 bunch fresh parsley
1 large bunch fresh basil
15 buffalo-milk mozzarella balls
2 16-ounce (1 l) bottles barbecue sauce
3 pounds (1.4 k) curly pasta, such as fusilli
2 20-ounce (500 g) boxes corn muffin mix
3 20-ounce (500 g) boxes brownie mix

Staples
Dijon mustard
Vinaigrette or other basic salad dressing

Tomato and Mozzarella Salad

10 large ripe tomatoes
15 mozzarella balls
1 large bunch fresh basil
Balsamic vinegar

1. Slice the tomatoes and arrange on a platter.

2. Slice the mozzarella and place a slice between each tomato slice.

3. Place a basil leaf between each slice of cheese and tomato. Drizzle vinegar over everything and let sit for at least an hour.

Preparation time: 15 minutes
Requires advance preparation

Pasta Salad

3 pounds (1.4 kg) curly pasta, such as fusilli
2 medium zucchini
2 medium yellow squash
2 yellow bell peppers
2 red bell peppers
1 bunch broccoli
12 cherry tomatoes
12 large mushrooms, sliced
¼ cup (5 g) chopped parsley
2 cups (500 ml) vinaigrette dressing
¼ cup (60 ml) Dijon mustard

1. Cook the pasta in boiling salted water until al dente, about 10 minutes. Drain, rinse, and set aside.

2. Slice the zucchini, summer squash, peppers, and broccoli into small pieces.

3. Put 2 cups (500 ml) of water into a saucepan and bring to a boil. Add the zucchini, squash, peppers, and broccoli and cook for 2 minutes. Remove from heat and drain.

4. Place cooked vegetables in a large bowl. Add the tomatoes and mushrooms and mix in the pasta. Stir in the parsley.

5. Blend the dressing and mustard, then toss into the salad. Serve at room temperature.

Preparation time: 20 minutes

Barbecued Chicken

60 pieces of chicken (wings, thighs, legs)
2 16-ounce (1 l) bottles barbecue sauce

1. Preheat the oven to 350° F (180° C).

2. Prepare a charcoal grill.

3. Place the chicken pieces in large baking pans and brush on sauce. Partly bake for 20 minutes. Then cook on a grill for another 30 minutes, brushing on more sauce as needed. (You can cook the chicken early in the day and serve it at room temperature.)

Preparation time: 1 hour

Corn Muffins

2 20-ounce (500 g) boxes corn muffin mix

1. Follow the directions on the box and make enough for 1 to 2 squares per person.

Preparation time: 25 minutes

Watermelon and Brownies

2 20-ounce (500 g) boxes brownie mix
1 large watermelon

1. Prepare the brownies according to package directions.

2. Slice the melon and arrange on a platter.

3. Arrange brownies on a tray and serve with melon.

Preparation time: 35 minutes

Snow Peas Stuffed with Seafood Salad

Barbecued Beef on Skewers   Mini Pesto Pizzas

Sesame Chicken Fingers   Skewered Marinated Tortellini

THE COCKTAIL PARTY

When I have the urge to entertain a large group of people but don't want to set up a big table for dinner, cocktails are the outcome. Indoors or out, it's a great way to catch up with friends.

1 pound (450 g) prepared seafood
  salad (from deli)
2 London broil steaks, about
  2 pounds (900 g) each
4 skinless and boneless whole
  chicken breasts
1 pound (450 g) snow peas
3 large tomatoes
2 garlic cloves
8 ounces (250 g) Parmesan cheese
  for grating
1 12-ounce (350 ml) bottle Italian
  dressing
1 10-ounce (300 ml) bottle teriyaki
  marinade
1 5-ounce (150 ml) bottle soy
  sauce
2 8-ounce (250 ml) jars pesto sauce
1 6-ounce (175 ml) jar honey
2 14-ounce (400 g) packages soft
  flour tortillas
1 4-ounce (115 g) package Italian-
  seasoned bread crumbs
1 3-ounce (85 g) box sesame seeds
2 1-pound (450 g) bags cheese
  tortellini
100 short wooden skewers

Staples
Curry powder
Pepper
Vinaigrette or other basic
  salad dressing

Snow Peas Stuffed with Seafood Salad

1 pound (450 g) seafood salad
2 tablespoons curry powder
1 pound (450 g) snow peas

1. Chop the seafood salad finely and add the curry powder.

2. Trim the strings from the snow peas. Open one side, creating a pocket, and fill with seafood salad. Refrigerate until serving.

Preparation time: 20 minutes

Barbecued Beef on Skewers

2 London Broil steaks, about
  2 pounds (900 g) each
1 cup (250 ml) Italian dressing
½ cup (125 ml) soy sauce
½ cup (125 ml) honey
2 garlic cloves, crushed

1. Mix the dressing, soy sauce, honey, and garlic and put into a pan.

2. Slice the steak into thin strips.

3. Twist the strips and slide onto skewers. Place in pan with marinade and let sit all day in marinade before grilling.

4. Prepare a charcoal grill.

5. When ready, grill the strips for 2 minutes on each side and serve.

Preparation time: 20 minutes
Requires advance preparation

Sesame Chicken Fingers

4 skinless and boneless
  chicken breasts
1 10-ounce (300 ml) bottle
  teriyaki marinade
½ cup (85 g) sesame seeds
Italian-seasoned bread
  crumbs

1. Preheat the oven to 350° F (180° C).

2. Slice the chicken breasts into ½-inch (1-cm) strips.

3. Dip the strips in teriyaki sauce and roll in sesame seeds and bread crumbs.

4. Bake on a cookie sheet for 25 minutes, or until chicken is white through to center.

Preparation time: 40 minutes

Skewered Marinated Tortellini

2 1-pound (450 g) bags
  cheese tortellini
Vinaigrette dressing
1 cup (125 g) grated
  Parmesan cheese
Freshly ground pepper

1. Cook the tortellini according to directions on bag, preferably a bit underdone.

2. Let cool and then place 3 tortellini on a wooden skewer. Repeat with remaining tortellini.

3. Place on a serving platter. Drizzle dressing, then sprinkle Parmesan cheese and pepper over the pasta and serve.

Preparation time: 30 minutes

Mini Pesto Pizzas

2 14-ounce (400 g) packages
  small flour tortillas
2 8-ounce (250 ml) jars pesto
  sauce
3 large tomatoes, chopped
1 cup (125 g) grated
  Parmesan cheese

1. Preheat the oven to 350° F (180° C).

2. Place the tortillas on an ungreased cookie sheet.

3. Spread a little pesto on each and sprinkle with tomatoes and Parmesan cheese. Bake for 12 minutes, or until bubbly.

Preparation time: 25 minutes

Butterflied Leg of Lamb   Green Beans with Rosemary & Parmesan

Cheese   Broiled New Potatoes   Blue Cheese & Walnut Salad

Strawberries & Blueberries with Mint

THE COOKOUT

When I think of summer, the first thing that comes to mind is cooking outdoors. Somehow, whatever you end up serving, eating outdoors always feels like a festive occasion.

SHOPPING LIST

1 leg of lamb, approximately
  5 to 7 pounds (2.2 to 3.2 kg),
  butterflied
4 large garlic cloves
1½ pounds (750 g) green beans
3 pounds (1.4 kg) small red
  potatoes
1 large head romaine lettuce
2 pints (900 g) cherry tomatoes
1 bunch fresh parsley
1 bunch fresh rosemary
1 bunch fresh mint
1 stick (115 g) butter
1 ounce (30 g) Parmesan cheese
  for grating
2 4-ounce (115 g) packages blue
  cheese
1 5-ounce (150 ml) jar soy sauce
12 walnuts
2 pints (400 g) strawberries
2 pints (400 g) blueberries
1 bunch fresh mint

Staples
Red wine vinegar
Olive oil
Dijon mustard
Olive oil
Vinaigrette or other basic
  salad dressing
Salt and pepper

Butterflied Leg of Lamb

¼ cup (60 ml) soy sauce
1 cup (250 ml) red wine
  vinegar
12 1-inch (2.5-cm) sprigs fresh
  rosemary
1 cup (250 ml) olive oil
¼ cup (50 g) chopped
  fresh mint
3 garlic cloves, crushed
⅛ cup (30 ml) Dijon mustard
1 leg of lamb, butterflied

1. Mix the soy sauce, vinegar, rosemary, olive oil, mint, garlic, and mustard in a bowl. Marinate the lamb for 4 to 6 hours.

2. When ready, prepare charcoal grill.

3. Drain and pat the meat dry, then grill to desired doneness, about 30 minutes for medium rare. Baste with marinade if desired.

Preparation time: 45 minutes
Requires advance preparation

Green Beans with Rosemary and Parmesan Cheese

¼ cup (60 g) butter
1 tablespoon chopped fresh
  rosemary
1 garlic clove, crushed
1½ pounds (750 g) green
  beans, boiled until tender
¼ cup (30 g) grated
  Parmesan cheese

1. Melt the butter and add the rosemary, garlic, and beans. Stir well to warm through, then remove from heat and add cheese and serve.

Preparation time: 45 minutes
Requires advance preparation

Broiled New Potatoes

25 to 30 small red potatoes, about 3 pounds (1.4 kg)
¼ to ½ cup (60 to 125 ml) olive oil
Salt and pepper

1. Preheat the oven to 400° F (200° C).

2. Cut the potatoes in half.

3. Pour the olive oil into a large baking dish, spreading evenly.

4. Place potatoes in baking dish cut side down, then sprinkle with oil, salt, and pepper.

5. Bake for 1 hour, or until potatoes are soft.

Preparation time: 1½ hours

Blue Cheese and Walnut Salad

1 large head romaine lettuce
2 4-ounce (115 g) packages blue cheese
12 walnuts, shelled and coarsely chopped
2 pints (900 g) cherry tomatoes
½ cup (10 g) chopped fresh parsley
Vinaigrette dressing

1. Wash lettuce and place in a large salad bowl. Crumble in the blue cheese and add the walnuts, tomatoes, and parsley.

2. Toss with dressing and serve.

Preparation time: 30 minutes

Strawberry and Blueberries with Mint

2 pints (400 g) fresh strawberries
2 pints (400 g) fresh blueberries
1 bunch fresh mint

1. Wash strawberries in cold water. Cut off stems and cut strawberries in half lengthwise and place in a bowl.

2. Wash blueberries in cold water and pull off all of the stems. Add to the bowl of strawberries.

3. Wash the mint and chop leaves into small pieces. Mix leaves with fruit and let mixture sit, covered, for an hour or so before serving.

4. Serve in a bowl or on a small plate with a cookie or whipped cream (or both!).

Preparation time: 15 minutes

Taco Salad & Chips   Make-Your-Own Fajitas

Spanish Rice   Lime Ice Cream Pie

THE REUNION

The phone rings and the next thing you know you have old friends coming to town that you haven't seen in ten years. This is just the excuse you were looking for to throw that offbeat little bash! Serve margaritas, which are easy to make if you use a mix.

SHOPPING LIST

3 pounds (1.4 kg) ground beef
4 skinless and boneless whole
  chicken breasts
6 medium tomatoes
6 large tomatoes
2 small bunches scallions
1 large onion and 1 small
2 heads iceberg lettuce
4 medium avocados
1 small lime
1 stick (115 g) butter
1 pint (500 ml) sour cream
8 ounces (250 g) cheddar cheese
2 1-ounce (30 g) envelopes taco
  seasoning
3 14-ounce (400 g) packages soft
  flour tortillas
2 12-ounce (350 g) bags corn chips
1 4-ounce (115 g) package quick-
  cooking brown rice
2 ½-ounce (15 g) boxes raisins
1 9-inch (23-cm) graham cracker
  crust
2 pints (1 l) vanilla ice cream
1 8-ounce bottle (236 ml) lime juice

Staples
Mayonnaise
Tabasco sauce
Red pepper

Taco Salad and Chips

3 pounds (1.4 kg) ground beef
2 1-ounce (30 g) envelopes
  taco seasoning
Flesh of 2 avocados
¼ cup (60 ml) mayonnaise
Dash of Tabasco sauce
1 head romaine or iceberg
  lettuce, shredded
2 cups (250 g) shredded
  cheddar cheese
6 medium tomatoes, chopped
2 small bunches scallions,
  chopped
Corn chips

1. Cook the ground beef in a frying pan with taco seasoning until no longer pink, about 10 minutes.

2. Mix the avocado, mayonnaise, and Tabasco until smooth.

3. Place the shredded lettuce on a plate. Arrange the ground meat, avocado mixture, cheese, tomatoes, and scallions in an attractive pattern and serve.

Preparation time: 30 minutes

Make-Your-Own Fajitas

4 skinless and boneless
  chicken breasts, cut into
  thin strips
1 large onion, chopped
2 tablespoons (30 g) butter
Flesh of 2 avocados
¼ cup (60 ml) mayonnaise
Dash of Tabasco sauce
2 cups (500 ml) shredded
  iceberg lettuce
6 large tomatoes, chopped
1 pint (500 ml) sour cream
3 14-ounce (400 g) packages
  soft flour tortillas

1. Sauté the strips of chicken and the onion in butter until chicken is golden brown, about 8 minutes. Set aside.

2. Blend the avocado, mayonnaise, and Tabasco until smooth.

3. Place the avocado, lettuce, tomatoes, and sour cream in separate bowls.

4. Warm the tortillas in the oven, then put on a plate and serve with the fillings.

Preparation time: 30 minutes

Spanish Rice

1 4-ounce (115 g) package
   quick-cooking brown rice
1 small onion, minced
1 red bell pepper, cored
   and diced
1 cup (30 g) raisins

1. Follow the instructions for cooking the rice on the package, but add the onion and bell pepper to the boiling water.

2. When the rice is done, stir in the raisins and serve.

Preparation time: 15 minutes

Lime Ice Cream Pie

1 9-inch (23-cm) prepared
   graham cracker crust
2 pints (1 l) vanilla ice cream
½ cup (125 ml) lime juice
1 small lime, thinly sliced

1. Soften the ice cream and place in a bowl. Stir in the lime juice, then spread in the crust as evenly as possible. Put back into the freezer until a few minutes before serving.

2. When serving, place a half-moon slice of lime on each pie slice.

Preparation time: 10 minutes
Requires advance preparation

RECIPE INDEX

INDEX OF INGREDIENTS

Seafood:
    casserole, 70
    salad, chicken stuffed with, 34
    salad, snow peas stuffed with,
        34
    skewered, 22
    spread, 16
Sesame:
    chicken fingers, 83
    noodles, 47
    pork loin, 46
Sherry:
    seafood casserole with, 70
    tomato soup with, 74
    winter squash soup with, 66
Shish-kebab. **See** Skewers
Shrimp:
    broiled, 50
    fettuccine with, 54
    seafood casserole with, 70
    skewered, 22
Skewers:
    barbecued beef on, 82
    marinated tortellini on, 83
    seafood on, 22
Snow peas, tortellini with, 30
Soufflé, spinach, 12
Soup:
    carrot, 26
    potato with chives, 46
    sweet potato, 58
    tomato, 74
    winter squash, 66
    zucchini, 54
Sour cream:
    beef stroganoff with, 12
    gazpacho with, 22
    spinach-artichoke casserole
        with, 18
Spinach:
    and artichoke casserole, 18
    beef tenderloin stuffed with, 67
    seafood casserole with, 70
    soufflé, 12
    tomatoes stuffed with, 13

Spreads:
    Havarti cheese, 50
    seafood, 16
    See also Dips
Squash:
    pasta salad with, 78
    rice medley with, 35
    soup, 66
    See also Zucchini
Strawberry and blueberry mixture,
    87
Stuffing:
    casserole with, 17
    wild rice, 59
Sweet potato soup, 58
Swiss cheese:
    asparagus with, 27
    broiled potatoes with, 67
    chicken casserole with, 17
    creamed onions with, 59
Teriyaki marinade, pork loin with,
    46
Tomato(es):
    avocado salad with, 75
    casserole with, 42
    fajitas with, 90
    garden salad with, 55
    mozzarella salad with, 78
    pasta salad with, 78
    sliced, with dill, 71
    soup, 74
    stuffed, 13, 31
    taco salad with, 90
    tortellini salad with, 63
Tortellini:
    marinated, on skewers, 83
    salad, 63
    wrapped with snow peas, 31
Tortillas:
    for fajitas, 90
    roast beef in, 75
Turnovers, blueberry, 13
Vegetables, marinated, 23
Vinaigrette dressing:
    avocado salad with, 75

breaded chicken breasts with, 62
    mixed green salad with, 47
    pasta salad with, 78
    pepper salad with, 66
    radish salad with, 19
    sliced tomatoes and dill with, 71
Walnuts:
    salad with, 31, 87
    wild rice with, 63
Watercress:
    salad, 31
    zucchini soup with, 54
Watermelon, brownies and, 79
Whipped cream, chocolate wafers
    with, 47
Wild rice:
    with grapes and rosemary, 31
    stuffing, 59
    with walnuts, 63
Wine, red:
    beef stroganoff with, 12
    pears cooked in, 23
    stuffed beef tenderloin with, 67
Wine, white:
    asparagus steamed in, 47
    chicken casserole with, 17
    crabmeat-stuffed chicken with,
        34
    creamed onions with, 59
    herbed potatoes with, 27
    stuffed cherry tomatoes with, 31
Winter squash soup, 66
Yellow squash:
    pasta salad with, 78
    rice medley with, 35
Zucchini:
    marinated, 23
    pasta salad with, 78
    rice medley with, 35
    soup, 54